JAGUARS

EYE TO EYE WITH BIG CATS

Jason Cooper

Rourke

www.rourkepublishing.com

PHOTO CREDITS: All photos © Lynn M. Stone.

Cover Photo: *As rare as they are beautiful, jaguars are the largest wild cats of the Americas.*

Editor: Frank Sloan

Cover design by Nicola Stratford

Library of Congress Cataloging-in-Publication Data

Cooper, Jason, 1942-
  Jaguars / Jason Cooper.
      p. cm. — (Eye to eye with big cats)
Summary: Describes the physical characteristics, habitat, and life cycle of jaguars.
Includes bibliographical references and index.
  ISBN 1-58952-403-9 (hardcover)
  1. Jaguar—Juvenile literature. [1. Jaguar. 2. Endangered species.]
I. Title.

  QL737.C23 C6748 2002
  599.75'5—dc21
                                                          2002003652

Printed in the USA

CG/CG

TABLE OF CONTENTS

THE JAGUAR

In 1500 the explorer **Amerigo Vespucci** was in South America. There he discovered jaguars, known as *Panthera onca*. Jaguars are one of the great meat-eating animals in the world.

The word jaguar comes from the language of a South American Indian tribe. Spanish-speaking Americans call the jaguar "el tigre."

"El tigre" prowls a forest in Belize, Central America.

THE JAGUAR'S RELATIVES

Jaguars are related to all cats. The jaguar has the typical cat, or **feline**, looks. It has the claws, teeth, blunt **snout**, and flexible body that all cats do.

The jaguar is most closely related to the leopard. Jaguars are spotted and have bodies like leopards'. And, like most of the big cats, jaguars make deep, coughing noises known as roars.

Leopards are the big spotted cats of Africa and Asia.

WHAT JAGUARS LOOK LIKE

A jaguar has a muscular body, a thick neck, and short, stout legs. Jaguars are stockier than leopards. A jaguar has spots known as **rosettes**. These spots are circular often with a black dot inside the circle. Leopard spots don't usually have a dot inside the ring. Most jaguars are brown with darker spots. However, black jaguars are fairly common.

Male jaguars usually weigh from 120 to 200 pounds (54 to 91 kilograms). Females average between 80 and 100 pounds (36 and 45 kilograms).

The jaguar's coat is similar to that of its cousin, the leopard.

WHERE JAGUARS LIVE

Jaguars live in much of South America and Central America. Sometimes they are found as far north as in parts of Mexico. Black jaguars are most common in the wet forests of Paraguay and Brazil.

The jaguar's home is known as its **habitat**. This habitat is often a wet tropical forest with a river or swamp.

Like leopards, jaguars enjoy resting in trees.

A black jaguar on the prowl

The jaguar is perfectly at home in the rain forest.

HOW JAGUARS LIVE

Like most cats, jaguars like to rest. They sharpen their claws and groom themselves. When they move, they walk. But they can be very fast when they need to be.

Jaguars usually travel and hunt alone, except for females with cubs. Most males keep to a small area known as their **territory**.

A sleepy jaguar naps in the midday heat of Central America.

JAGUAR CUBS

Baby jaguars can be born any time of the year in South America. A litter will have one to four cubs. They are born near bushes, rocks, or trees.

Cubs feed first on their mothers' milk and then on meat she brings to them. They begin to follow their mothers when they are just six weeks old. It will be several months before they hunt on their own. They depend on their mothers for about two years.

A jaguar cub looks out from its rock perch.

PREDATOR AND PREY

In its own territory the jaguar is a powerful **predator**, or hunter. It hunts by **stalking** other animals, its **prey**. Most jaguars hunt at night. They have excellent sight and hearing.

A jaguar usually creeps along toward its prey. But a jaguar will also climb trees and splash into water. The jaguar has very strong jaws. It often kills by biting through its prey's skull.

The tapir is one kind of prey for the jaguar.

19

JAGUARS AND PEOPLE

Jaguars are both feared and respected by the natives of South and Central America. Some early people thought jaguars were gods. Jaguars have been the subject of many legends.

Jaguars rarely attack humans. Jaguars are often killed for their fur, which is sometimes in great demand. Today, they are mostly found in zoos.

A black jaguar stalks prey.

THE FUTURE OF JAGUARS

South American countries have begun to protect their jaguars. In 1984, the Central American country of Belize opened a park for the safety of jaguars. And the trade in fur has slowed down.

But jaguars are losing their land. Much of their habitat is being turned into farms. Farmers often kill jaguars because they attack their livestock. **Poachers** still shoot some jaguars. Poachers are people who hunt against the law. All these things mean the jaguar is an **endangered species**.

GLOSSARY

endangered species (en DANE juhrd SPEE seez) — in danger of no longer existing; very rare

feline (FEE line) — of the cat family

habitat (HAB uh tat) — the area in which an animal lives

poachers (POH churz) — people who hunt against the law

predator (PRED uh tor) — an animal that kills another animal for food

prey (PRAY) — an animal that is hunted for food by another animal

rosettes (roe ZETZ) — round spots with a black dot in the center

snout (SNOWT) — an animal's nose

stalking (STOCK ing) — hunting by slowly and quietly moving toward the victim

territory (TARE uh TOR ee) — a home area defended by certain animals that live within it

Vespucci, Amerigo (VEZ pooh chee, Ah MEHR uh go) — an Italian explorer of the 1500s

INDEX

Further Reading

Coleman, Melissa S. *Jaguars and Leopards*. Blackbirch, 2002
Lalley, Pat. *Jaguars*. Raintree Steck Vaughn, 2001
Woods, Theresa. *Jaguars*. Child's World, 2001

Websites To Visit

http://www.primenet.com/~brendel/jaguar.html
http://dspace.dial.pipex.com/agarman/jaguar.htm

About The Author

Jason Cooper has written several children's books about a variety of topics for Rourke Publishing, including recent series *China Discovery* and *American Landmarks*. Cooper travels widely to gather information for his books. Two of his favorite travel destinations are Alaska and the Far East.